TWINKLING

By Twink E. Twinkle and Mary Lynne Berard

A Rescued Pug Dog's Self-Learned Guide
on How to Become a **STAR**

Archway Publishing books may be ordered through booksellers or by contacting:

Archway Publishing
1663 Liberty Drive
Bloomington, IN 47403
www.archwaypublishing.com
1 (888) 242-5904

ISBN: 978-1-4808-6957-8 (sc)
ISBN: 978-1-4808-6956-1 (e)

Print information available on the last page.

Archway Publishing rev. date: 12/18/2018

~ AUTHOR'S FOREWORD ~

Encouraged by others, to share what worked for us by retraining our mind, spirit and bodies, from thinking and communicating negative thoughts, words and deeds into **positive** attitudes and actions.

Within our "TWINKLING" self-learned, twenty-one days. training guide, we will show you how you can retrain your mind, your dog's mind, as well as your friends, for a successful finish.

We desire for your inner light to shine as brightly as ours', which is why we have name our self-learned training guide, "TWINKLING."

It is our sincere hope that through our "TWINKLING" self-learned guide, you too, will find your predestined purpose for your life.

For me, Twinkle, I have found what matters most, after years of feeling nobody wanted me in their lives. What I have found is the complete feeling of unconditional **love** for me from Mary Lynne.

For Mary Lynne, she has found the complete feeling of unconditional, loyal **love** from a Pug dog named, Twink E. Twinkle.

Our feelings of unconditional love have **elevated** and **motivated** us to bring **love** and **joy** into the hearts of all we meet daily.

It's Time to Learn **"TWINKLING"**

With Me, Twink E. Twinkle

Waiting on my first day of therapy dog training.

~ TABLE OF CONTENTS ~

Practicing teaching others dogs to become therapy dogs too!

~ INTRODUCTION ~
"TWINKLING" EXERCISES – SEVEN STEPS PREPARATION ON: HOW TO TRAIN THE TRAINOR

This "Twinkling" self-learned training guide offers a successful, simplistic, logical formula to train oneself on how to train a dog, based on a true story.

You will learn how to **train yourself first**, and then, in turn, your dog, based on consistent discipline to desire, to find, and set a goal in your, and your dog's life. You will learn how to work as a team effort.

The following 21- day sequence of training events will be your consistent, **repetitive** formula to achieve desired results in finding and meeting your goal.

Below are your suggested successful training techniques, that worked for Mary Lynne and Twink E. Twinkle that helped us prepare, and then, reach our goal, as a successful certified therapy dog partnership team.

1. Select a favorite place that will help you **relax** for your **visual meditation** training exercises. You might also like to play soft meditation music.
2. Seek **spiritual** guidance for your **visual** meditation, which will **clear** your **mind of distractions**; concentrate on what is your goal in your life?
3. **Learn** and practice **SLOW** deep breathing exercises; 10 times, 2x daily.
4. Seek **spiritual** guidance to **find your negative thoughts** (scars). **Write them down, then trash them**.
5. Select a **positive affirmation**(s) that will **convince** your mind on your Goal choice.
6. **Vocalize** your goal affirmation(s) 10 times in a mirror, 2x daily.
7. **Discipline** and **commitment** on following your exercises is required, **practice 2x daily**.

INTRODUCTION: TRAIN THE TRAINER PREPARATION, CONTD.

1. To start your training exercises, **find** a quiet location whereby you can **feel relaxed daily. Select** a **comfortable chair or training** mat, to begin your **visual meditation**. You might also play quiet, meditation background music to help you relax your muscles.

2. Suggest you seek **spiritual** (your higher power) guidance, through prayer, to **ask for guidance** in finding your **life's purpose, believing** you were born to be blessed.

3. **Begin** your **SLOW deep breathing** exercises to create relaxation by sending more oxygen to your brain. **Breath in slowly** through your nose, mouth closed, until your lungs can't take in more air, **hold** your breath for three (3) seconds, then **breath out VERY SLOWLY** through your pursed lips. The **key is breath in slowly, breath out slowly**. This process will clear your mind, which will bring you inner peace.

4. Again, through spiritual guidance, **ask to have your negative thoughts (scars) in your brain revealed to you**, while still practicing your deep breathing. **Write down**, on a piece of paper what negative thoughts that have been revealed to you.

5. Upon completion of writing down your negative thoughts, then again, through seeking spiritual guidance, **ask that your thoughts/scars be removed from your brain**. Next, tear up what you have written down and **put them in a trash can**. You have **now trashed your negative thoughts** in preparation of reprogramming your mind with **positive thoughts**.

6. Seek spiritual guidance again to **ask for positive thoughts** to enter your brain and spirit, to **help** you **find** your goal in life. **Write** your **positive thoughts down**, then **start vocalizing out loud** these thought, as an **affirmation(s), in a mirror**, ten times each, practice twice daily.

7. **Discipline** and **commitment** to these exercises is a **must to succeed**. Practice **twice** daily.

~ CHAPTER ONE ~
Getting to Know Us
"TWINKLING" EXERCISE. #1

MEMORIES OF ADOPTION DAY

MARY LYNNE AND "TIMMY"

~ CHAPTER ONE ~
MARY L. BERARD AND TWINK E. TWINKLE'S
TRUE STORY

Now let's get to the good part when I met Mary Lynne. We both have grown so much together and have so much in common. We both have overcome bad situations in our lives.

When Mary Lynne was four years old, she was seriously burned playing in the basement while her mother was upstairs cooking Thanksgiving dinner. An old-fashion gas hot water heater exploded, igniting her nylon robe with fire, giving Mary Lynne intense pain.

This was her first experience with negative emotions. After an extended hospital stay, upon returning home, Mary Lynne caught Scarlet Fever, which aggravated Mary Lynne's extensive burns. Because Scarlet Fever is contagious and deadly, Mary Lynne and her mother were quarantined, and her father and brother had to leave the home.

Soon Mary Lynne began to slowly recover. During her father's first visit to see her, he noticed that Mary Lynne and her mother were acting sad. Mary Lynne explained to her father that she wanted to go and play outside. The doctor told her she could not go out and risk having the illness return.

Mary Lynne had toys to play with, but what she really needed was a living friend to be with. As her father left from one special visit, he knew exactly what Mary Lynne needed to lift her spirits… a warm, furry pet! The next time Mary Lynne's father came to see her, he surprised Mary Lynne with a Boston Terrier puppy. Mary Lynne was so happy to have a live little friend with a heartbeat. The puppy was already named "Tiny Tim McGinty", because he was so small, however Mary Lynne later nicknamed him "Timmy".

With the arrival of Timmy, Mary Lynne and her mother's spirits were uplifted with joy. Their lives began to change! Timmy became their baby to care for. Timmy was better than any toy, because he was alive, happy to be loved and give back love to Mary Lynne and her mother, who were still quarantined.

Mary Lynne began to recover rapidly because joy and a new form of love had entered her life. Timmy and Mary Lynne became the best of friends, until Mary Lynne became a young woman and Timmy passed away, after 12 years at Mary Lynne's side.

Through this painful childhood experience, Mary Lynne learned the power of having a pet, to offset the negative emotion of pain and loneliness. Many years later, she learned about pet therapy to help heal the sick and elderly. Mary Lynne was excited to use this method to help others the way Timmy had helped her.

After Mary Lynne had retired from her work, it became possible to build her dream of helping others through pet therapy. She began to search for a rescued Pug dog to adopt, since she felt another Boston Terrier could NEVER replace her memories and love for Timmy.

The search began for a young, healthy Pug dog that Mary Lynne could train to serve as her pet therapy team partner. Three weeks later a rescued Pug dog, (me, Twink) was recommend for consideration for adoption; for reasons I am confused about, I was labeled as a problem. They said I had an aggressive personality, when I was just trying to keep that other cruel dog from eating my food!

Mary Lynne was not sure about adopting me, when she heard that nobody was interested in a dog with behavior issues; however, Mary Lynne decided to try me out. The rescue team leader sent Mary Lynne my picture, and after viewing me, gratefully, Mary Lynne ACCEPTED me. I mean how could she not?!

The adoption process moved quickly after my new home was approved.

When Mary Lynne arrived at my foster home to pick me up, I was confused. I didn't want to leave my brother, who had to stay behind. When Mary Lynne and her granddaughter drove off with me, I cried like a baby the whole way to my new home.

Mary Lynne's granddaughter comforted me during this long journey. When we arrived at my new home, I was given a new name, "Twink." Mary Lynne said, "that my full name would be Twink E. Twinkle, but that I had to earn my middle name, which stands for "Exceptional." I had no idea what was in store for me.

I did not know what to make of my new home. Bowls of food and water were placed on the floor for me. I couldn't eat because I was nervous and scared. After a while, I settled in and ate. After dinner, Mary Lynne went to bed and I hopped in with her. I felt safe and right at home! I could not understand why the adoption team said that I was a problem dog? But with Mary Lynne's unconditional love for me, I would learn to turn my emotional scars into twinkling **STARS**!

So now, my new friends, with the help of Mary Lynne, I have prepared a special self-help guide just for you. Through this guide, you too can turn your emotional, painful scars into a **STAR** performance too!

~ CHAPTER TWO ~
BEHAVIOR MODIFICATION TRAINING
"TWINKLING" EXERCISE, #2

Introduction: Train the Trainor Preparation.

1. To start your training exercises, find a quiet location whereby you can feel relaxed daily. Select a comfortable chair or training mat, to begin your visual meditation. You might also play quiet, meditation background music to help you relax.

2. Suggest you seek spiritual (your higher power) guidance, through prayer, to ask for guidance in finding your life's purpose, believing you were **born to be blessed**.

3. Begin your **SLOW** deep breathing exercises to create relaxation by sending more oxygen to your brain. Breath in slowly through your nose, mouth closed, until your lungs take in more air, hold your breath for three (3) seconds, then breath out VERY SLOWLY through your pursed lips. The key is breath in slowly, breath out slowly. This process will clear your mind after seeking your spiritual guidance, which will bring you inner peace.

4. Again, through spiritual guidance, ask to have your negative thoughts (scars) in your brain revealed to you, while still practicing your deep breathing. **Write down,** on a piece of paper what negative thoughts that have been revealed to you.

5. Upon completion of writing down your negative thoughts, then again, through seeking spiritual guidance, tear up what you have written down and put them in a **trash can**. You have now **trashed** your negative thoughts in preparation of reprogramming your mind with **positive thoughts.**

6. Seek spiritual guidance again to ask for positive thoughts to enter your brain and spirit, to help you find your goal in life. Write your positive thoughts down, then start **vocalizing** out loud these thoughts, as an affirmation, in a **mirror**, **ten times** each, twice daily.

7. Discipline and commitment is a **must** to **succeed**. Practice **twice daily**.

It was less than one month since I had arrived at Mary Lynne's house, and oh bow wow, do I remember that day well! I had just finished my morning meal when Mary Lynne spoke to me and said, "Twinkle, today is the day that we are going to start our new beginnings."

I was confused, I thought I had already started my new beginnings in my new home, where I felt safe and enjoyed learning "how" to be loved. From the tone of Mary Lynne's voice, I was worried. I thought that I had done something wrong! Terrible thoughts raced through my mind, would I have to leave the home where I was finally felt being loved? Mary Lynne noticed the scared look in my eyes. In my heart, I knew she could sense my worried feelings.

Instead of getting ready for our morning walk, I began to hide in my bed. That's when Mary Lynne said to me, "no, you can forget your bed Twinkle, today is the day that you will start healing your bad memories." In a commanding positive tone, she exclaimed; "Today is your first training day Twinkle. Today is a time of new positive beginnings for you! You must believe that wonderful things happen in small beginnings, and that you, Twinkle, were created and born to be blessed."

Hearing Mary Lynne's positive voice brought excitement into my heart. I too felt that something good was planned for me.

On my **first day** of training, Mary Lynne got my leash, then we walked to the front door, for what I thought was going to be my fun morning walk. Mary Lynne said: "Twinkle, now is the time to change those stinking thinking negative thoughts into positive thoughts." Instead of a leisurely morning walk filled with listening to the birds and trying to chase squirrels, I was in for a big shocking surprise.

Something happened to my sweet, gentle, Mary Lynne, who in the past would let me do what I wanted on our walks together. Mary Lynne's behavior had changed. She would no longer let me be an untrained dog. She guided me on my leash, instead of me guiding her, no longer allowing me to walk in front of her or change sides without her permission. The days of chasing those pesky squirrels, cats and dogs were over!

My leash was in Mary Lynne's complete control. When I would try to do what I wanted, I learned very quickly by Mary Lynne's jerking on my leash and collar, that I was doing something wrong. Oh, what a shock! At the end of my walk, I learned that this was **day one**, of my twenty-one-day training program!

Day two: The same leash-collar walking program, however a new training lesson took place. I was being trained to come to Mary Lynne when she called my name. This was hard for me to understand, but Mary Lynne made it easy. After many times of being called to her side, when I finally responded to my name, and came to her. My reward was a wonderful, delicious dog treat, that Mary Lynne had in hand.

For the next hour, we practiced, and I was rewarded repeatedly. I was so happy to please Mary Lynne and receive my treats. I could have practiced my lesson all day.

Day three: Same leash-collar training and me responding to my name when I was called. However, this was another special day, I learned another new command! I learned to "sit and stay." It was easier to practice this training, since I could smell the dog treats in Mary Lynne's pocket from the previous training day, so I knew something good was coming my way.

Again, we practiced responding to my name and then, the "sit and stay" command. Mary Lynne was so pleased with me. She gave me so much love and praise, along with all those delicious treats.

Day four: We practiced my routines from days one, two, and three, but I still wanted to learn more! Just as I had hoped, Mary Lynne taught me another new command! Mary Lynne placed one of my yummy dog treats right in front of where I was sitting on the floor, oh what torture! What could this mean?

I then heard Mary Lynne's commanding voice say, "leave it". When I started to bend down and eat the treat, I heard Mary Lynne's voice say "leave it" again. I looked at Mary Lynne, she knew I was trying to obey her command and she responded with "good girl, Twinkle," and then she let me eat the treat. We then repeated this lesson again and again.

Day five: Practiced the previous days training commands, and again learned a new one; how to perform a little dance on my hind legs. Thanks to Mary Lynne's guidance, after many tries, I was finally able to dance for her as she sang a special song to me. Mary Lynne was so thrilled with my progress that my doggie spirit was filled with more love and happiness than I ever thought possible!

Day six: After practicing my new commands, Mary Lynne kneeled to me and said: "Twinkle, your progress has been nothing short of amazing, you're smart and I can see it in your eyes, you want to be a star!" After hearing the wonderful words of encouragement from Mary Lynne, I thought for the first time in my life, maybe I could be in a dog show some day!

She said that in a dog show, I would need to learn how to pose for a "judge's review," and that she would show me how to do it. Like usual, I had no trouble learning this command. As we ended day six of training, I felt so proud of myself! While it started out hard, learning was becoming fun!

Day seven: Mary Lynne said to me: "Twinkle, today is the day you learn how to pray and give thanks for achieving so much, in such a brief time." She showed me how to stretch out on the floor, how to put my head down between my front legs and paws, and how to mentally pray. When people saw me doing my praying, some cried, many wanted to hug and kiss me, so I am doing a lot of praying now-a-days in front of people.

I close my Behavior Modification Training chapter with this thought. Although my training sessions were hard for me initially, I know in my dog brain that love elevates, love motivates, and love creates! Mary Lynne was right when she said: "I was born to be blessed," but my joy now comes from being a blessing to others.

~ CHAPTER THREE ~
GOAL SETTING PROGRAM
"TWINKLING" EXERCISE, #3

STEP 1:

Visit your local library, bookstore, or online retailer to find **GOAL SETTING** literature that **inspires** you!

STEP 2:

Read at least **10 pages** a day to set a routine for **success**!

STEP 3:

Create an **ACTIVITIES BOARD** to layout different ideas and steps you can take towards your **GOAL!**

GOAL SETTING PROGRAM

STEP 4:

Be CREATIVE! Write down all your GOALS and **place** them on your ACTIVITIES BOARD. **Look** at this every **morning** when you start your day to focus your mind on the things to work on to get you closer to your GOAL!

Mary Lynne felt it was now time for me to change my old negative behavioral habits. Mary Lynne knew it was now my time to set new positive goals after my lack of training and bad aggressive habits I picked up from the old foster home.

It was first explained to me, so that I could start to emotionally grow into my dog-driven purpose, that negative thoughts and habits do not go away, they always remain until you change your underlying unpleasant habits.

What I learned from my basic training skills is repetition, going over and over a command, and then rewarded with tasty dog treats. What I loved most of all was receiving Mary Lynne's loving praises and hugs when I performed my commands correctly. Remember love elevates, love motivates, love creates, and when you add a tasty dog treat you become an achiever!

After successfully trashing my formerly negative behavior, I became eager to please Mary Lynne with my new good habits. She always rewarded me with treats, so that I would remember wonderful things start with small beginnings.

My daily learning and practices of my basic behavior modification training became positive energy for me. I looked forward to learning my positive new commands. It did not take 21 days of training for Mary Lynne to tell me it was time for me to set my goal for my dog-driven purpose in making people happy. Mary Lynne told me that my goal would be a credentialed pet therapy dog. "Umm…"

I wondered exactly what would I be doing? Mary Lynne could read my thoughts and promptly told me that we both would become credentialed to serve as a volunteer pet therapy team, Mary Lynne, my handler and I, her pet therapy dog.

As I was paying attention to Mary Lynne's serious tone of voice, Mary Lynne was instructing me. She said that without setting goals in our life, we do not have a map to guide us-- thus, we simply go in circles, without getting to our destinations." We both must achieve our goals together. Let's go and get started!

Mary Lynne, being my responsible owner was fully prepared with her training guide to instruct me on what I must learn to pass the difficult tests ahead of me. First, my canine health records had to be up-to-date and my grooming acceptable. We did not waste any time on getting started with mastering the various test categories. Mary Lynne set her goal to have me ready for my first test in just one month. It was for passing the American Kennel Club's Canine Good Citizen (CGC) test of 10 commands listed here. Test 1: Accepting a friendly stranger. Test 2: Sitting politely for petting. Test 3: Appearance and grooming. Test 4: Out for a walk (walking on a loose lead) Test 5: Walking through a crowd. Test 6: Sit and down on command and Staying in place. Test 7: Coming when called.

Gratefully, I passed and received a beautiful American Kennel Club Canine Good Citizen (CGC) certificate and CGC title next to my name.

The additional tests included the basis AKC, CGC 10 commands, required more training not only for myself, but for my responsible owner Mary Lynne, who was required to pass a comprehensive training program for admittance to hospitals, nursing home, schools or any public certified visits.

Whereas my additional testing required no barking, cause for immediate disqualification; commands of staying with a strange evaluator, no treats given to the dog to force commands, walking in the mix with other strange dogs, no reaction to loud voices or other noises, and not eating a treat placed in front of dog until given a command to eat it.

The purpose of Mary Lynne and Twinkle's volunteer animal pet therapy mission together was to visit hospitals, special needs centers, schools, and nursing homes to bring love, joy, happiness, and a feeling of well-being to people young and old alike.

Since I love to be loved, this new goal made me feel happy! Mary Lynne told me that when I reach my certification goals, I will have a dog-driven and purposeful life! Instead of just eating, sleeping, and living a boring life at home. My main goal would be to make people happy each day!

At the end of my 21st day of training, I was happy to report that I am ready to take my first of three certification tests. Through Mary Lynne, I learned that love elevates, love motivates, and love creates!

On the 30th day of the month, I successfully passed my first certification test! Mary Lynne congratulated me with a big doggie, treat along with hugs, kisses, and lots of happy praises.

Then Mary Lynne said to me "Twinkle, see how love elevates, love motivates, and love creates--you are now on your way to live and enjoying your dog-driven purposeful life!"

Twinkle Practicing Her Mirror Affirmation Goal

~ CHAPTER FOUR ~
TWINKLE REACHING OUR PRIMARY GOAL
"TWINKLING" EXERCISE, #4

STEP 1:

THINK....
Select one **POSITIVE** goal every day!
(**Write** in your goal below)

_____

_____

_____

_____

STEP 2:

COMMIT!
Say "**I WILL**" **practice** my exercises and **work** towards my goal **DAILY**!"
(Write in your commitment to practice below)

_____

_____

_____

_____

STEP 3:

VISUALIZE
Draw a picture below on what **achieving your goal looks like to you**!

STEP 4:

AFFIRMATIONS
(Refer to Chapter Seven for suggestions, write down below)

Look in the mirror, vocalize and **visualize** yourself **achieving** your **GOAL**!

_____

_____

_____

_____

Waking up and feeling happy from the joy of passing my Saturday test, little did I know that the second phase of my goal training was just ahead of me today. Mary Lynne was up early and, of course, so was I on another wonderful Monday morning.

I was gobbling down my breakfast when I heard the jiggling of my leash. Oh good, Mary Lynne and I will enjoy an early morning walk! Little did I know that I was to learn more commands today! Mary Lynne having been trained over the years to meet her goals, became my taskmistress. She learned from her experiences that although you can set your goals, it sometimes becomes difficult accomplishing them.

Even though I am a dog who can't read or write, I can hear and understand my instructions, and my spirit was motivated to please Mary Lynne. I felt happy and energized learning how to meet my goals that Mary Lynne outlined for me. And oh yes, I loved all the yummy reward treats I received while learning too! My joy was knowing what I had to do, to reach my goals for Mary Lynne. I knew what steps I had to take to become the driven dog I aspired to be.

So, my friends, think about what you want to accomplish in your life, your goal(s). Write them down and visualize yourself meeting your goal(s). What sort of things are you doing? Can you notice things you shouldn't be doing in your life that may be hindering your progress? Visualizing your success, reflecting on your previous actions, and truly believing you were born to be blessed will be your keys to success!

This is what I have learned so far in my training. Mary Lynne knew that a positive mind-set creates happiness, good health, enthusiasm, and instills a positive outcome in everything you want to achieve.

Mary Lynne and I were ready to master the second and third levels of my certification training goals. We were in this together in mind, body, and spirit.

This time the training commands were even more challenging. I would not say I wanted to "quit", since I heard over and over from Mary Lynne that "quitters never win, and winners never quit!" I was not allowed to show the negative emotion of self-pity. I wanted to WIN; and I too wanted my praises and yummy treats from Mary Lynne when I remembered my commands!

Mary Lynne was concerned that with the winter weather was fast approaching, our daily outside training exercises might need altering. We pushed on and ramped up our training to meet our next scheduled testing date. To move my story along, in less than one month, I, along with my handler, were-tested on the second phase of our pet therapy credentials.

Here are some of the new test requirements, I can't remember them all, but these were the hardest for me:

The additional tests included the basis AKC, CGC 10 commands, required more training not only for myself, but for my responsible owner Mary Lynne, who was required to pass a comprehensive training program for admittance to hospitals, nursing home, schools or any public certified visits.

Whereas, my additional testing required no barking, cause for immediate disqualification; commands of staying with a strange evaluator, no treats given to the dog to force commands, walking in the mix with other strange dogs, no reaction to loud voices or other noises, and not eating a treat placed in front of dog until given a command to eat it.

After all our challenging work to beat the weather, congratulations were in order! I passed my second phase test! Even though I would like to receive all the credit for my demanding work, it could not have been achieved without Mary Lynne's guidance. It was Mary Lynne's driving force that enabled me to turn my negative emotional scars into a star performance.

~ CHAPTER FIVE ~
HOW WE DID IT!
"TWINKLING" EXERCISE, #5

STEP 1:

Repeat, Repeat… REPEAT!
Repetition is the key to achieve your GOAL.

MEDITATION + SLOW DEEP BREATHING + AFFIRMATION = SUCCESS!!!

STEP 2:

Be Accountable!
Review your daily planner / calendar. Did you miss a day?

STEP 3:

Personalize!
Go ahead, name and write down your first goal book below:

_____

_____

_____

_____

STEP 4:

Organize!
Write out your daily exercise schedule to achieve your GOAL!

_____

_____

_____

_____

After reading how "I did it", it is now time to start finding and reaching your goals. I suggest that you find a quiet spot, perhaps outside while looking at the heavenly stars, and start meditating and visualizing on who you are, and what is your purpose in the book of life.

When you have a thought that makes you feel happy, then start your planning, like Mary Lynne did for me.

The previous **"TWINKLING"** exercises will help you get started: (Below is your check list to review).

Meditation for inspiration on finding your goal - (Example, I want to be a doctor, nurse, athlete etc.) Write down what inspire your below.

_____

_____

_____

_____

Setting a goal - (**Write down** what you want to be in your book, titled: My life).

_____

_____

_____

_____

Read on what you need to get started - (Education preparation).

Write down your **daily** vocal affirmation: "I will be...": (write your goal here).

_____

_____

_____

_____

While **looking in a mirror, say out loud** your goal and **your daily affirmation**, at least 10 times a day. (Refer to Chapter Seven for affirmation suggestions.)

Keep a daily record on how you are progressing on reaching your goal. (Example: It was easier for me to learn what it takes for me to reach my goal).

After 21 days check and review your progress. YOU WILL BE AMAZED! You will see that you are on the way to **stardom**!

~ CHAPTER SIX ~
HERE IS HOW!
"TWINKLING" EXERCISE, #6

STEP 1:
BELIEVE!
I **WILL** think positive thoughts.
I **CAN** and I **WILL** achieve my **GOAL**!!!

STEP 2:
Throw out the **NEGATIVE**!
Take all your negative thoughts about yourself and write
them down; then throw **them in the TRASH**!!!
(**Believe in yourself!**)

STEP 3:

Find Inspiration!
Remember, go to your local library, bookstore, or internet retailer and find a
book that **inspires you to follow your dreams and achieve your GOAL**!!

STEP 4:

COMMIT to your GOAL!
Tell yourself "I **WILL** make a 21-day training plan, and I **WILL**
work everyday on my exercise to **achieve** my **GOAL**!

OK, it is time for you to think what are your "stinking thinking of negative thoughts," and then, put them into the trash can. Here's my suggestion. Write out your negative thoughts, for example, "I can't do this, it is too hard for me"; or, "I need so much equipment to be an athlete." These are negative thoughts.

Now go throw them away in a trash can. Now that you have done that, write out your positive thoughts to replace in your brain, example: First step, stop and slowly take a deep breath through your nose, then say out loud, while you are exhaling: Yes, I **CAN** and **WILL** be: (**say your goal here**).

By following the above steps, you will begin your positive replacement formula that is: **Recognize, Replace and then Receive.** Repeat the **slow** breathing exercise ten times. You will then feel **positive** energy surging through your spirit, mind and body.

Remember my friends, we were created to be blessed for your individual, pre-destined, purpose driven life. The fun begins discovering what your purpose driven life will be! It will not be easy at first, because you will have to change your unpleasant habits by replacing them with good ones.
Your life will become an adventure. You will create a book on your adventure, like mine today. Think of your experience in finding your predestined purpose driven life, like going on a treasure hunt.

Be assured, you will find the prize is within you, as you become more energized in reaching your goal. Why wait another minute starting your most important lifetime venture in easily solving one of life's most important mysteries! **Strive to answer this question: "Who am I, and what is my purpose in life**?

~ CHAPTER SEVEN ~
WHAT IS YOUR GOAL?

Ok, no more Twinkle's chapter titles, it is **now your time** to document your goal.

(Select **Your** Own Title: **Now That You Can Do It!**)

Please write down in this chapter how you accomplished your goal. Keep this chapter for sharing, as a keepsake, to review repeatedly, on how you became a **STAR** by practicing your **"Twinkling"** goal setting exercises.

(Access suggested affirmations to recite on **reverse side below):** Write **down** your favorite one(s) below.

_____

_____

_____

_____

Hugs and kisses and all best wishes, as you start your and your dog's **new adventure in finding your predestined purpose driven life, together.**

Twink E. Twinkle and Mary Lynne

SUGGESTED AFFIRMATIONS THAT HELPED
TWINK E. TWINKLE AND MARY LYNNE REACH THEIR GOAL

I WAS CREATED TO BE BLESS IN REACHING MY GOAL.

I CAN REACH TO THE STARs BY HEALING MY SCARs.

LOOSERS NEVER WIN, WINNERS NEVER LOSE.

TO REACH MY GOAL, I MUST SPEAK IT TO REACH IT.

I MUST BELIEVE IT TO ACHIEVE IT.

I CAN, AND I WILL, REACH MY GOAL (SPEAK WHAT YOUR GOAL IS).

I MUST BELIEVE IN MY GOAL TO ACHIEVE IT.

IN MY MIRROR, THE ME I SEE, IS THE ME I'LL BE, IF I BELIEVE.

FOR YOUR NOTES

Printed in the United States
By Bookmasters